The Essential Air Fryer Cookbook

Affordable, Delicious and Healthy Recipes for Everyone
incl. Low Carb Bonus

[1st Edition]

Leo Parker

TABLE OF CONTENTS

Appliances in the kitchen are there to help cooks prepare foods easily and quickly. With eating trends turning towards ingredients that are healthy as well as tasty, it is no wonder that manufacturers have turned their attention to fabricating appliances that keep nutrition locked in. Nowhere is this better demonstrated than with the growing popularity of the air fryer.

A kitchen appliance that cooks foods through circulating heated air by means of a convection mechanism, the air fryer can be found on countertops in every home where nutrition, taste, and convenience are valued. Not only are air fryers compact and durable, but they are rapidly replacing the microwave oven as the must-have kitchen appliance of the future.

Air fryers are more than just a handy gadget to have in the kitchen for emergencies. An air fryer combines many essential food preparation methods - such as browning and roasting - cooking techniques that impart more flavour to the food while locking in the nutrition. Many households are ditching the microwave and embracing cooking with an air fryer for these reasons.

For many years, the air fryer stayed the secret of professional eating establishments and large hotel chains. Now, air fryers hold the position as one of the fastest growing favourite kitchen appliances in the world.

What is an Air Fryer & How Does it Work?

The air fryer was originally developed in 2005 by Turbochef Technologies for the hotel and restaurant industries. Philips utilised patented "Rapid Air" technology in 2010 to create the Airfryer, an appliance for use at home. As of the last quarter of 2019, there are many brands of air fryer on the market available at different price points. Even though the countertop air fryer is the perfect alternative to other traditional oil frying methods, it has alternate applications besides replacing deep or shallow frying techniques.

Every air fryer has a mechanical fan used to circulate heat around the food at supercharged speeds. This cooks the food, and also creates two kinds of browning reactions. A caramelisation occurs from the sugars in the food breaking down and chemically transforming into crisper, darker complex substances at temperatures between 110° and 180°C. Additionally, there is a Maillard reaction that produces brown ring compounds. The Maillard reaction cause these flavourful compounds to bind together upon exposure to temperatures between 140° and 165°C.

How traditional frying methods work is by inducing the Maillard effect by submerging foods into hot oil completely. This is what causes the proteins, fats, and sugars to crisp and brown. Because water only boils to a maximum capacity of 100°C, it can never produce the Maillard and caramelisation techniques. Microwaving agitates the water content of foods to cook them, and this is why meats cooked in the microwave turn grey and not brown. Air fryers work by coating the foods in thin layers of oil, and circulating the hot air. This initiates the browning reaction. Not only does an air fryer use 70 to 80% less fats and oils than traditional deep and shallow frying techniques, but it can crisp up delicious edibles such as crumbed chicken steaklets, burgers, chips, pies, and biscuits with significantly reduced calorie content.

Air fryers are a healthy alternative to traditional deep fried ingredients. They allow a far healthier eating plan, but still includes frying, grilling, and baking. Most air fryers have timer and temperature adjustments for more precise cooking styles. Air fryer use has been developed to be simple and easy. Once the basic settings, cooking methods, and maintenance have been mastered, any home cook can place the chosen ingredients in a basket device on top of the drip tray, and wait for the food to be cooked. Some air fryer models have to be shaken occasionally to ensure the oil coverage is even. Other makes and brands have a food agitator incorporated into the fryer that does this automatically.

After the ingredients have been lightly coated in oil, the air fryer fan circulates the hot air that is radiating from the heating element next to the food. This means the oil coating is superheated and fries, grills, or bakes the food the way the dietary preferences of the chef dictates. There is an opening at the top of the fryer and also an air outlet at the back, and these should never be obstructed.

Using an air fryer helps cut much of the fat content out of fried foods while retaining the ingredients nutritional content. Statistics have indicated that up to 75% of the fat found in fried foods is eliminated when using an air fryer. This is because deep fryers need 50 times more oil to operate efficiently compared to an air fryer. Many deep-fried recipes call for approximately 750ml of oil as opposed to an air fryer using only one tablespoon. One study showed that air-fried chips and deep-fried chips had the same colouration and moisture content, but significantly less fat was found in the air-fried chips. This can have a big effect on health, nutrition, and diet, as a dense fat intake from certain vegetable oils and the way the product is manufactured has been associated with an increased risk of inflammation and heart disease.

Air Fryer Maintenance

Air fryers are so easy to cook with and simple to use. These features, in addition to the incredible convenience of being able to prepare healthier food options, means an air fryer will always be on the countertop ready for meals and menus every day. However, this appliance won't last forever without proper maintenance and cleaning. There are some important guidelines to keep in mind to ensure the air dryer functions at optimal levels and remains a useful, productive appliance for many years.

Upon opening and unpacking the air fryer, it is recommended you read the manufacturer's manual before setting up and air frying with your new appliance. The instructions laid out by the manufacturers are there to keep the appliance in optimum working order. Begin by reading through how to clean your air fryer. In the past, deep frying any food could turn into a greasy mess, but air fryers are very different. The cooking basket that comes with the appliance is completely enclosed, and this eliminates any splatters and drips. There is an oil pan that catches the drips below, and this makes cleaning a lot easier.

Cleaning an air fryer after every use is still the best way to prolong its lifespan. Always unplug the appliance from the wall plug and allow it to lose heat first. You can then begin wiping the outside exterior with a clean, damp cloth. Next, remove the pan, basket, and tray from the air fryer before washing and rinsing in hot water with a dishwasher soap, such as Fairy. The removable components in an air dryer are all dishwasher safe and can be put in the dishwasher appliance if preferred.

Following the removal and cleaning of the detachable parts, it is time to clean the air fryer inside with a cloth or sponge that has been dipped into hot water, and wrung out. If any food is stuck to the heating element positioned above the food basket, simply clean if off with a soft brush. Before you put the basket, tray, and pan back into the air fryer, be sure to dry them thoroughly with a non-fluff cloth.

When the air fryer is clean, store it safely in an upright position when it has cooled down, and unplug it from the wall socket. Some fryers have storage compartments to house the cord. Although regular cleaning, as well as operating the fryer on a sturdy, flat surface is both essential air fryer maintenance, there are still a few checks to do before using your appliance every time.

Begin by checking the cord for damage or fraying. Remember to clean the cord after use and store it without kinks and bends. If you only plan to use the air fryer occasionally, check for dust and old accumulated food before switching it on. The surface on which you place the appliance must be level and steady. It must never be placed directly against another appliance or wall, as air fryers require a minimum of 10cm/4" of space above and at the sides. If the appliance is not able to vent hot air and steam while cooking, it can cause the appliance to overheat.

It's a better idea to use some of these handy tips and tricks for air fryer maintenance. Never use an ordinary kitchen utensil to remove any food that has become embedded or stuck on to the air fryer components. Each piece in the appliance has been coated with non-stick coating similar to Teflon, and this makes it easy to scratch. It's important to use a non-abrasive sponge or cloth to remove the stuck-on food residue found on the drip pan or basket.

If the food residue has hardened on the pan, tray, and basket, try soaking them in warm water with dishwasher soap added to it. The heat will soften the food after soaking, and this makes it much easier to remove with a sponge or cloth. When you are air frying consecutive batches of food one after the other, it's best to wait until the final batch is cooked before removing the components for cleaning.

If your air fryer manages to retain the odours of the foods you have been cooking in it, this is very easily remedied. The best method is by washing the components immediately after use. If the smell continues to linger after washing according to instructions, try leaving the basket and pan in hot water and add a mild dishwasher soap for approximately one hour, and then clean it again. You can also neutralise food undesirable odours by swiping a cut lemon over the removable components or squeezing it onto a paper towel and wiping the air fryer down with it. Leave for thirty minutes and rinse.

The components of an air fryer are covered in a harmless non-stick coating. If this coating is accidentally scratched by a sharp utensil, it could cause the non-stick coating to bubble up and peel. If you see any of the components have begun to peel or bubble, contact customer service if your air fryer is still under warranty.

If you experience any difficulty sling the pan component into the air fryer, this means there is too much food in the air fryer basket. A quick fix is to remove some of the food items and cook the meal in two batches. Check the basket as well, as it might not have been properly attached to the pan. Try lifting the basket clear of the pan and inserting it back in again. There will always be a solid "click" sound to alert you that the components are in correctly.

If you see white smoke coming out of the pan while cooking, this is caused when too much grease or oil has pooled in the drip pan. This usually happens if the air fryer was put away before cleaning or in between batches of cooking foods such as bacon or sausages. The smoke doesn't cause damage; all you have to do is unplug the air fryer, allow it to cool, and wipe off the grease.

If you find that the food is frequently undercooked or raw in some places and not others, this is an indication that too much food has been put into the cooking basket. The heat generated by the coil is only being absorbed by the top layer of the food, and is not able to penetrate deeper. Because of the percolating manner of the air conduction, improperly cooked food will be the result when the ingredients have been crammed into the basket too tightly. Try cooking smaller batches, as this permits better air circulation.

If you have setup your air fryer and found that it isn't turning on, check to see the electricity outlet is properly connected before calling a repair service or the manufacturer. If the electrical plug is switched on and you are up to date with maintaining the components according to the recommended guidelines, the problem is most likely to be mechanical. Contact your manufacturer to set you up with a qualified repair service. It's great idea to bookmark the manufacturer's website page when you first buy your air fryer. In this way, you will always have their contact details on hand if you need to contact them in case of a mechanical failure.

You will enjoy creating nutritious, delicious, faux-fried foods in your air fryer. This nifty new appliance is set to become a kitchen staple for years to come

Time: 20 minutes | Amount: 4 egg and ham toast cups

Ingredients:

- ◆ 4 ramekins or similar small ovenproof pots
- ◆ 4 eggs
- ◆ 8 slices toast in bread of your choice
- ◆ 2 slices ham (tomato for vegetarian option)
- ◆ Melted butter
- ◆ Salt, pepper
- ◆ Cheese (optional)
- ◆ Preheat Airfryer to 160ºC

Preparation:

1.	Brush ramekins inside with lots of melted butter.
2.	Flatten the toast slices with your hand or rolling pin.
3.	Line the ramekins with one slice of toast, then place the second slice on top. Push in firmly until they line the ramekin.
4.	Cut ham into strips, and line the ramekin interior in a circle.
5.	Break one egg in the ramekin toast and ham "nest."
6.	If you are using cheese, sprinkle on grated cheese now.
7.	Sprinkle seasoning over.
8.	Place 4 ramekins in the fryer for around 15 minutes or so at 160ºC.
9.	Remove from pots by running a knife around the edge.
10.	If you prefer your eggs runnier, cook for 12 mins, and harder, then cook for 18 mins.

Time: 20 minutes | Amount: Serves 2

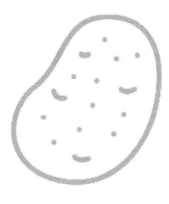

Ingredients:

- 3 jumbo eggs
- ½ chorizo sausage sliced
- 1 large potato, peeled and cubed
- 125ml frozen corn
- Olive oil
- Chopped herbs of your choice
- Feta to sprinkle
- Salt and pepper
- Set air fryer to 185ºC

Preparation:

1.	Pour a good glug of olive oil into air fryer pan, add chorizo, corn, and potato cubes.
2.	Cook in air fryer until slightly browned.
3.	Beat all the eggs in a bowl, and season with salt and pepper.
4.	Pour eggs over the potato, corn, and chorizo. Sprinkle with feta and herbs.
5.	Bake another 5 minutes, and then check firmness and continue for a bit longer if you prefer your frittata well done.
6.	Turn frittata onto a serving dish and decorate with rocket and tomato relish.

Time: 15 minutes | Amount: Serves 2

Ingredients:

- 2 medium potatoes cut up into pieces (the smaller the cubes, the faster they cook)
- Olive oil
- Salt and pepper
- 1 bell pepper sliced up
- 1 onion diced
- Set air fryer at 200°C

Preparation:

1.	Put potato cubes in a round bowl pour over enough olive oil to coat the potatoes by shaking the bowl.
2.	Set timer for 8 minutes and cook potatoes - giving the basket a shake and stir half way through.
3.	Place chopped bell peppers and onions into bowl, coat with a little olive oil Add to basket and fry for a further 8 minutes.
4.	Check ingredients are cooked through, and give them another 5 minutes if they have too much bite. You may need to give the basket a toss after two minutes.
5.	Season and serve.

Time: 30 - 40 minutes | Amount: 8 croquettes

Ingredients:

- ◆ 4 potatoes, peeled and grated
- ◆ Corn flour
- ◆ Salt and white pepper
- ◆ 10ml Chilli flakes
- ◆ 5ml garlic powder (optional)
- ◆ Onion powder (optional)
- ◆ Vegetable oil 5ml + another 5ml

Preparation:

1.	Cover grated potato with cold water, soak, and rinse. Repeat until water is clear (2 – 3 rinses).
2.	Heat 5ml of oil in a saucepan and sauté potatoes for three to four minutes.
3.	Transfer potatoes to a plate, cool, and then put in the corn flour, seasoning, garlic and onion powders if using, and chilli flakes. Mix together roughly and refrigerate.
4.	Heat air fryer to 190ºC while waiting for potatoes to cool.
5.	Take potatoes out of the fridge, and divide into 8 pieces.
6.	Brush air fryer basket with remaining 5ml oil.
7.	Place croquettes into basket and air fry for 15 minutes.
8.	After 6 minutes, take basket out and turn croquettes over. Fry until done (another 5 mins)
9.	Serve hot with brown sauce or tomato sauce.

Time: 20 minutes | Amount: Serves 2

Ingredients:

♦ 4 slices of bread – any kind

♦ 30ml softened butter or margarine

♦ 2 eggs

♦ Pinch salt

♦ Pinch nutmeg

♦ Pinch ground cloves

♦ 5ml icing sugar

♦ Maple syrup to serve

♦ Preheat air fryer to 180ºC

Preparation:

1.	Gently beat the eggs with cinnamon, cloves, and nutmeg.
2.	Spread butter or marge on both bread slices, and cut into strips.
3.	Put strips in the egg mix, and then into fryer (cook in two batches).
4.	After two minutes or so, pause the fryer and check on the cooking.
5.	Bake a further 4 minutes. Check to see they don't over-brown.
6.	When both batches are finished, sprinkle with icing sugar, drizzle with maple syrup, and serve immediately.

Time: 40 minutes | Amount: 9 doughnuts

Ingredients:

- ♦ 125ml white sugar
- ♦ 60ml room temperature butter
- ♦ 2 egg yolks
- ♦ 575ml all-purpose flour
- ♦ 7.5ml baking powder
- ♦ 5ml salt
- ♦ 125ml sour cream
- ♦ 80ml caster sugar + 5ml cinnamon for dusting
- ♦ 30ml melted butter for basting
- ♦ Preheat air fryer to 175ºC

Preparation:

1.	Whisk 125ml sugar and butter until combined. Add egg yolks and mix further.
2.	Sift together flour, BP, and salt in a different bowl. Add a third of the flour mix and half the sour cream into the sugar + egg mix, and hand beat until combined. Continue to hand mix in the remaining sour cream and flour until a dough is formed.
3.	Combine caster sugar plus cinnamon in a bowl
4.	Roll out dough onto a floured dusted surface until approximately 1.5cm thick. Cut 9 circles out of the dough, and poke a finger hole into the centre of each one.
5.	Brush half the melted butter over both sides of the doughnuts.
6.	Place half the doughnuts into the basket, and cook for 7 minutes. Remove doughnuts from the basket, brush the remaining doughnuts with the butter on both sides, and cook for 8 minutes.
7.	When first batch is out of the fryer and the second batch is cooking, dust first batch liberally with sugar and cinnamon mix. Do the same with the second batch when they are cooked. Serve hot.

Time: 25 minutes | Amount: 2 servings

Ingredients:

- 2 large sweet potatoes (orange flesh or white flesh)
- 125ml bacon pieces
- 60ml oil like olive oil
- 30ml paprika
- 5ml sea salt or Kosher salt
- 5ml ground black pepper
- 5ml fresh or dried dill
- Preheat fryer to 200ºC

Preparation:

1.	Toss sweet potato, bacon bits, olive oil, paprika, salt, pepper, and dill together in a round bowl.
2.	Place mix into the air fryer.
3.	Cook for 12 to 16 minutes. Check mix after 10 minutes and give ingredients a toss if needed.
4.	Take out and serve hot when crispy and brown.

Time: 15 minutes | Amount: 2 to 4 portions

Ingredients:

- ◆ 1 packet sausage patties or 1 tray of sausages
- ◆ 1 non-stick cooking spray
- ◆ Preheat air fryer 200ºC

Preparation:

1.	Place sausage patties into basket after spraying both sides with non-stick spray.
2.	If you are using sausages instead, simply squeeze meat out of the casing, form into patties, and spray.
3.	Cook in the preheated air fryer for 4 minutes. Pull the basket out, turn patties to the other side, and cook for another few minutes until baked through. Take out and serve hot with tomato sauce. Cook in batches if you need to.

Time: 30 minutes | Amount: Serves 4

Ingredients:

- ♦ 1 sheet frozen and thawed puff pastry
- ♦ 120ml grated Cheddar cheese
- ♦ 120ml diced and cooked ham
- ♦ 4 eggs
- ♦ Chopped chives (optional)
- ♦ Preheat air fryer to 200°C

Preparation:

1.	Cut pastry sheet into squares (4).
2.	Place two of the squares in the basket, and cook for up to 8 minutes.
3.	Remove basket from the air fryer and use a metal spoon to press an indentation into each one gently. Into this hollow, place 15ml cheese, 15ml ham, (a small amount that fits into the cupped palm of your hand), and pour one egg on top.
4.	Return to fryer, and cook until eggs are perfect to taste. If you enjoy your eggs runny, check after 4 minutes.
5.	Repeat with second batch.
6.	Allow tarts to cool for 2 to 3 minutes before serving sprinkled with chives.

Time: 8 minutes | Amount: Serves 4

Ingredients:

- 2 eggs beaten
- 80ml milk
- Pinch salt
- Chopped meat and vegetables of your choice.
  Some good ones are bell pepper, ham, spring onion, and mushrooms.
- Chopped chives (optional)
- 80ml grated cheese
- Preheat air fryer to 180ºC

Preparation:

1.	Mix up the eggs and milk in a round bowl.
2.	Add a little salt, and mix further.
3.	Add veggies.
4.	Pour the egg mix into a non-stick pan, and place in the basket.
5.	Cook for up to 10 minutes according to taste. Check on the cooking halfway through and when you do this sprinkle some cheese over the top.
6.	Use a thin, non-metallic spatula to loosen omelette for the pan, and transfer to plate.
7.	Garnish with spring onions if preferred.

Time: 45 minutes | Amount: 1 loaf serves 8

Ingredients:

♦ 175ml whole wheat flour

♦ 5ml cinnamon

♦ 2ml fine salt

♦ 1.5ml baking soda

♦ 2 ripe bananas, mashed

♦ 2 large eggs, beaten

♦ 125ml sugar

♦ 80ml plain, non-fat yogurt

♦ 60ml oil

♦ 5ml vanilla extract

♦ 60ml chopped walnuts (optional)

♦ Cooking spray

♦ Preheat air fryer to 160ºC

Preparation:

1.	Line a 16cm cake tin with baking paper.
2.	Lightly coat with non-stick spray.
3.	Sift together flour, cinnamon, salt, and baking soda, and set aside.
4.	In a separate round bowl, whisk together bananas, oil, the vanilla, the eggs, and sugar.
5.	Gently stir wet ingredients into the flour mix until combined.
6.	Pour batter into the baking tin, and sprinkle walnuts on top.
7.	Place banana bread mix pan into the air fryer, and cook until browned and a skewer comes out without batter on it when inserted into the middle, around 30 minutes.
8.	Transfer bread to a wire cooling rack to cool in the tin for a few minutes.
9.	Slice and serve.

WHITE BREAD

Time: 2 hours | Amount: serves 8

Ingredients:

- ◆ 300g all-purpose flour
- ◆ 60ml honey
- ◆ 60ml condensed milk
- ◆ 5ml Kosher salt
- ◆ 1 sachet instant yeast powder
- ◆ 1 small egg, beaten
- ◆ 150ml cold milk
- ◆ 30ml olive oil

Preparation:

1.	Sift together flour and salt. Add yeast sachet.
2.	Mix the beaten egg and cold milk together, and add condensed milk and honey. Add this combination to the flour mix.
3.	Knead to a dough with a dough hook or with a wooden spoon.
4.	Mix in olive oil, knead ingredients together on a flat surface until dough has been worked to a smooth shine.
5.	Rest in a warm place in a bowl covered with a damp tea towel, until roughly double in size.
6.	Preheat air fryer to 160°C.
7.	Knock the dough back, knead again, and rest for about 14 minutes.
8.	Place in a well-oiled pan or tin.
9.	Brush bread dough with water, scatter over with sesame seeds, or any other bread seed to taste, and then bake in the air fryer for 20 minutes.

Time: 40 minutes | Amount: serves 4

Ingredients:

- ♦ 750ml whole wheat flour
- ♦ 5ml baking soda
- ♦ 5ml sea salt
- ♦ 30ml sugar
- ♦ 60ml butter, cubed into small pieces and chilled
- ♦ 1 large egg, beaten
- ♦ 375ml buttermilk
- ♦ Preheat air fryer to 350ºC

Preparation:

1.	Combine whole wheat flour and baking soda together in a large bowl.
2.	Add butter straight from the fridge and mix into flour using a fork or pastry blender until the mix resembles breadcrumbs.
3.	Make a dip in the centre, and add the eggs and the buttermilk.
4.	Mix together well with a wooden spoon until it forms a wet, sticky dough.
5.	Coat hands in flour and work the dough mix into rough ball. Turn onto a well-floured surface and gently knead it lightly. Form it into a rough ball shape. Do not over-knead.
6.	Score an X onto the top surface of the dough, and carefully transfer dough into a well-greased air fryer basket.
7.	Bake for around 28 minutes before inserting a skewer into the middle to see if it comes out without dough on it. If the skewer is still wet, continue to bake at 5 minute intervals until the skewer comes out clean.
8.	Place on wire rack to cool.
9.	Serve with jam and butter or as an accompaniment to soups and stews.
10.	Mix mango, lime juice, gin, ginger beer, sugar and ice cubes into a puree.

Time: 1 ½ hours | Amount: serves 4

Ingredients:

- 125ml whole wheat flour
- 125ml white flour
- ½ sachet instant yeast powder or 3.5g from a 7g sachet
- Round cake tin with low sides or 15cm diameter pizza pan

Preparation:

1.	Mix flours together with salt, yeast, and seeds.
2.	Add 150 to 200ml warm water while mixing slowly.
3.	When soft dough forms, knead for 7 minutes until the dough becomes smooth and elastic.
4.	Place dough mix in a greased bowl, cover with damp cloth (not wet) and leave to prove in a warm space for around 30 minutes.
5.	Preheat air fryer to 200°C, and brush the dough on top with water.
6.	Place the loaf tin on top of the fryer basket, and bake for 22 minutes or until golden and hollow sounding when tapped.
7.	Cool down on a wire rack, and serve with butter.

Time: 8 hours proving the dough | 25 minutes to air fry | Amount: Serves 4

Ingredients:

- 250ml sourdough starter (available at good shops and bakers)
- 250ml unbleached all-purpose flour
- 75ml whole wheat flour
- 30ml sugar
- 2.5ml sea salt
- 30ml olive oil

Preparation:

1.	Mix everything together, and then run it on the bread mixing and kneading setting if you are using a mixer. If you are doing it by hand, knead and fold the dough until it becomes silky and is no longer sticky to the touch.
2.	Remove the paddles from the mixing bowl and allow the dough to rise for four hours or in the fridge overnight.
3.	Transfer the dough to a well-greased bowl or purpose-made proofing basket, and leave to rise for a further three hours in a warm place.
4.	Preheat air fryer to 195ºC, and flip the dough out of the bowl onto the grill component of the air fryer. Brush the grill very lightly with oil first.
5.	Air fry for 20 to 25 minutes, checking half way to give the bread a gentle shake. Tap before taking out of the air fryer to hear a nice, hollow sound.
6.	Transfer boule to wire rack, and wait 2 hours before slicing.

Time: 35 minutes | Amount: 4 servings

Ingredients:

- 1 large egg
- 500g boneless, skinless chicken thighs, patted dry and cut into 5cm chunks
- 80ml cornstarch + 10ml
- 1.5ml kosher salt
- 1.5ml ground white pepper
- 120ml low sodium chicken stock
- 30ml low sodium soy sauce
- 30ml tomato sauce
- 10ml sugar
- 10ml rice vinegar
- 25ml canola oil
- 3 Thai chillies, chopped and deseeded
- 15ml freshly grated ginger
- 2 – 3 diagonally sliced spring onions
- 5ml toasted sesame oil
- 5ml toasted sesame seeds
- Preheat air fryer to 200ºC

Preparation:

1.	Beat the fresh egg in a large bowl and then add the chicken pieces. Coat well.
2.	In another round bowl, combine 10ml cornstarch with salt and pepper. Transfer the chicken to the cornstarch bowl and stir together with a spatula until every piece is coated.
3.	Transfer chicken pieces to the oven racks on the air fryer, or the fryer basket. Remember to leave space in between the pieces.
4.	Cook for 12 to 16 minutes in the air fryer, giving it a shake midway. The chicken pieces are ready when crispy all over.
5.	Allow the pieces to sit for 5 minutes after leaving the oven, and then whisk together the 10ml cornstarch, chicken stock, soy sauce, tomato sauce, sugar, and rice vinegar. Heat oil to a medium temperature in a cast iron frying pan on the stovetop.
6.	When chillies are sizzling, add the aromatics (garlic and ginger) and cook until fragrant.
7.	Rewhisk the cornstarch mixture and stir into the frying pan. When mix begins to bubble and thicken, take it off the hob and add to the chicken pieces.
8.	Serve with brown or white rice and top off with sesame seeds and spring onion.

Time: 45 minutes | Amount: Makes 24

Ingredients:

- 30ml olive oil
- 1 finely chopped shallot
- 3 garlic cloves minced
- 60ml Panko breadcrumbs
- 30ml milk
- 375g beef mince
- 175g turkey/ostrich/chicken mince
- 1 large egg, beaten
- 80ml chopped flat leaf parsley
- 15ml finely chopped rosemary
- 15ml finely chopped thyme
- 15ml Dijon mustard
- 2.5ml kosher salt
- Preheat air fryer to 200ºC

Preparation:

1.	Heat the oil in a non-stick or Teflon pan over a medium to high heat. Add shallot and cook until transparent. Add garlic, stir for one minute and remove from heat.
2.	Combine Panko bread crumbs and milk in a round bowl, and stand for 6 minutes.
3.	Add shallots and garlic to Panko mix, then add minces, herbs, mustard, and salt. Stir to combine.
4.	Shape mix into 3cm diameter balls and place in one layer in the fryer basket. Cook in batches with space in between the balls. Each batch will cook through in 10 to 12 minutes. Remove each batch when done, and keep warm.
5.	Serve meatballs with noodles or spaghetti and homemade tomato sauce poured over. Also good in a sub sandwich.

ITALIAN-STYLE MEATBALLS

Time: 25 minutes | Amount: 1 serving

Ingredients:

- ♦ 250g bone-in centre cut pork chop
- ♦ Cooking spray
- ♦ 0.5ml kosher salt
- ♦ 2.5ml black pepper
- ♦ 5ml olive oil
- ♦ 5ml maple syrup
- ♦ 5ml Dijon mustard
- ♦ 175g Brussels sprouts
- ♦ Preheat air fryer to 200ºC

Preparation:

1.	Lightly coat chop with cooking spray, dust with salt and half the black pepper. Whisk oil, syrup, mustard, and rest of the pepper together in a medium round bowl.
2.	Wash, peel, and halve Brussels sprouts and coat in oil and syrup mix.
3.	Place chop on one side of the fryer basket, and the coated sprouts on the other.
4.	Air fry until the chop is cooked through and the sprouts are a light gold, which will take about 8 or 10 minutes for medium done and 13 minutes for well done.

Ingredients:

- ◆ 15ml oil (olive or canola)
- ◆ 100gmince beef
- ◆ 1 medium onion, diced up into small pieces
- ◆ 100g finely chopped mushrooms
- ◆ 2 cloves of fresh garlic, crushed
- ◆ 2 de-pitted green olives, chopped
- ◆ 1ml paprika
- ◆ 1ml cumin powder
- ◆ 0.5ml cinnamon powder
- ◆ 125ml chopped tomatoes
  (about 3 small or2 large red and ripe
  tomatoes)
- ◆ 8 square gyoza wrappers
- ◆ One egg, beaten
- ◆ Preheat air fryer 200ºC

EMPANADAS

Preparation:

1.	Heat canola or olive oil over medium heat in a cast iron frying pan on the stovetop. Add onion and garlic aromatics, and stir lightly for 2 or 3minutes, then set it aside. Add mince, brown until it begins to separate and crumble, then add the mushrooms. Stir until the moisture released from the mushrooms has disappeared and the mushrooms have started to brown, about 6 to 8 minutes. Add onion and garlic mix, olives, paprika, cumin, and cinnamon. Cook until all ingredients have combined and then add the tomatoes. Cook for one or two minutes while stirring gently, and then transfer the mix to a bowl. Allow to cool down for 6 minutes.
2.	Place wrappers on work surface and fill the centre of each wrapper with 20ml – 25ml filling (about one and half tablespoons). Brush wrapper edges with egg, fold wrappers over, and pinch the edges firmly to seal.
3.	Place 4 empanadas – one batch - in one layer in the fryer basket, and cook until brown and golden (about 7 minutes). Repeat.
4.	Serve this dish while warm with a salsa dip.

Time: 40 minutes | Amount: Serves 2

Ingredients:

- 10 large chicken wing drumettes (upper part of the wing)
- Cooking spray
- 15ml rice vinegar
- 50ml honey
- 30ml low sodium chicken stock
- 15ml low sodium soy sauce
- 15ml toasted sesame oil
- 2ml chilli flakes
- 1 clove garlic, crushed
- 30ml low salt, roasted peanuts
- Small bunch fresh chives, chopped
- Preheat air fryer 200ºC

Preparation:

1.	Place clean and dry drumettes in a single layer in the air fryer basket, coat them lightly with non-stick spray, and bake until the skin is crispy (about 30 minutes).
2.	Stir together the vinegar, the honey, chicken stock, soy sauce, oil, chilli flakes, and crushed fresh garlic in a cast iron frying pan and wait for it all to cook on a medium-high heat on the stovetop. Simmer until mix thickens (6 minutes).
3.	When drumettes are fully cooked, remove them from the fryer and coat them in the honey mixture. Sprinkle with peanuts and chives, and serve with chips or mash potato.

Time: 35 minutes | Amount: Serves 2

Ingredients:

- 4 highest quality hot dogs
- 4 bamboo skewers
- 2 eggs, beaten
- 250ml crushed cornflakes
- Cooking spray
- Mustard and tomato sauce
- Preheat air fryer to 190ºC

Preparation:

1.	Insert a skewer into one end of the hot dog.
2.	Place flour into a glass or ceramic dish or plate. Put beaten eggs into a second shallow dish. Finally, place the cornflakes into another shallow dish. Dredge hot dogs in flour, shake off the excess flour and dip the hot dog into the egg. Immediately coat hot dog in cornflakes crumbs, you can press down with your hands to make the flakes stick if some fall off.
3.	Coat air fryer with cooking spray. Place corn dogs in basket, spray them cooking spray, and bake until brown and golden and crunchy (about 10 minutes). Turn dogs half way through cooking.
4.	If the hot dogs and skewers are too long, cut in half and air fry in batches.
5.	Serve with chips and relishes.

Time: 7 hours | Amount: Serves 4

Ingredients:

- ◆ 500ml buttermilk
- ◆ 5ml paprika
- ◆ 2.5ml cayenne pepper
- ◆ 4 boneless, skinless chicken thighs
- ◆ 250ml all-purpose flour
- ◆ 2 eggs, beaten
- ◆ 30ml water
- ◆ 500ml Panko or any Japanese-style breadcrumbs
- ◆ 2.5ml kosher salt
- ◆ Cooking spray
- ◆ Hot sauce to taste

Preparation:

1.	Combine the buttermilk, the paprika, and the cayenne in a large bowl. Add thighs and coat. Cover with plastic cling wrap and refrigerate for 6 hours minimum or overnight.
2.	Preheat air fryer to 200°C.
3.	Place flour mix in a shallow, flat dish and the beaten eggs in another. Put Panko on a flat plate. Remove thighs from marinade and discard the remaining marinade. Lightly salt thighs, dredge in flour, and then shake off excess coating Now, dip into egg mix and immediately dredge in Panko. You can use your hands to press the mix on firmly. Spray thighs with cooking spray on all sides.
4.	Spray basket with non-stick spray and put highs into the basket in one layer. Cook in batches until chicken is crispy and golden brown (16 minutes). Turn thighs over half way. Check chicken temperature is 100°C when a thermometer is inserted.
5.	Serve with hot sauce and rice.
6.	Turn frittata onto a serving dish and decorate with rocket and tomato relish.

Time: 1 hour | Amount: serves 4 - 6

Ingredients:

- 5ml canola oil
- 375g bok choy
- 15ml freshly grated ginger
- 3 crushed garlic cloves
- 175g pork mince
- 2ml chilli flakes
- 18 – 24 dumpling or wonton wrappers
- Cooking spray
- 30ml rice vinegar
- 30ml soy sauce
- 5ml toasted sesame oil
- 3ml light brown sugar
- Small bunch chopped spring onions
- Preheat air fryer to 190ºC

Preparation:

1.	Heat oil in cast iron pan over medium or medium high heat. Add bok choy and wait until it is wilted and dry. Add aromatic ginger and garlic and stir until mixed. Transfer the vegetable to a bowl and cool. Pat mixture dry with a few sheets of paper towel.
2.	Combine pork, bok choy mix, and red chilli flakes in a medium sized round bowl.
3.	Place wrapper on work surface and fill with 20ml – 25ml of filling (one tablespoon). Moisten the edges of the wrapper, fold over and pinch closed with your fingers to make a half moon shape. Repeat.
4.	Lightly coat air fryer with cooking spray and place 6 dumplings in the basket. Spray dumplings with cooking spray and cook until light brown in colour 912 minutes) turning half way through. Keep first batches warm.
5.	Stir the rice vinegar, the soy sauce, sesame oil, sugar, and chopped spring onions together in a small round bowl until combined.
6.	Serve dumpling with the dipping sauce on the side.

Time: 30 minutes | Amount: Serves 2

Ingredients:

- ♦ 2 x 175g – 250g room temperature steaks cut 2cm thick and patted dry
- ♦ 5ml olive oil to coat
- ♦ 2ml garlic powder (optional)
- ♦ Sea salt
- ♦ A few twists of black pepper from a pepper mill
- ♦ Butter
- ♦ Preheat air fryer to 200ºC

Preparation:

1.	Lightly coat steaks with oil. Season the steaks to taste with the salt and black ground pepper on both sides.
2.	Place the steaks in basket and air fry for 8 to 18 minutes according to how you like your steak done. Flip steaks half way through.
3.	Put a knob of butter on each steak when it comes out of the air fryer, cover with foil, and allow steaks to rest for 10 minutes.
4.	Serve with salads and baked potatoes.

Time: 25 minutes | Amount: 1 – 2 servings

Ingredients:

- ◆ 1 – 2 lamb chops
- ◆ 15ml finely chopped garlic
- ◆ 15ml finely chopped rosemary
- ◆ 50ml canola or olive oil
- ◆ salt

Preparation:

1.	Mix rosemary, fresh garlic, and canola or olive oil together in a small round bowl, and place the chops in the marinade while you heat up the air fryer to175ºC.
2.	When the air fryer has reached the desired temperature, place the chops in the lightly oiled basket and cook for around 10 to 25 minutes, depending on if you like well done or medium cooked lamb.
3.	When the chops have come out the air fryer, allow the chops to rest for 8 to 10 minutes before serving with mash potatoes and red wine jus.

Time: 30 minutes | Amount: serves 2

Ingredients:

- 500g cod, cut into 4 evenly sized pieces
- Kosher salt
- Freshly ground black pepper
- 125ml plain flour
- One egg, beaten
- 500ml Panko breadcrumbs
- 0.5ml celery salt
- 0.5ml paprika
- o.5ml cayenne
- 0.5ml dry mustard powder
- A tiny pinch of nutmeg
- Lemon wedges for serving
- Tartar sauce
- Preheat air fryer to 200ºC

Preparation:

1.	Pat fish pieces dry and season.
2.	Place egg, flour, and Panko in three separate bowls. Add the celery salt, paprika, cayenne, dry mustard powder, and pinch of nutmeg to the Panko and combine.
3.	Individually coat each fish piece in flour, then dip in egg, and finally cover in the Panko. Press the coating gently to firm it up.
4.	Working in batches, place the fish into the air fryer basket, and cook for 8 to 12 minutes, turning over halfway through. Wait until the fish batter is golden before removing.
5.	Serves with lemon wedges, chips, and tartar sauce.

Time: 25 minutes | Amount: serves 2 to 3

Ingredients:

- 500g shrimp, raw, peeled, and deveined
- Cooking Spray
- 2ml garlic powder
- Salt
- Black pepper
- Lemon wedges to serve
- Chilli flakes/parsley (optional)
- Preheat air fryer to 200ºC

Preparation:

1.	Toss the prepared shrimp in a bowl while spraying with the cooking oil. Add the seasoning and garlic powder, and toss again to coat evenly.
2.	Add shrimp to the air fryer basket in one layer.
3.	Cook for 10 to 14 minutes, flipping halfway through by tossing the basket.
4.	When shrimp are pink and cooked through, transfer them to a bowl and squeeze over some lemon.
5.	Serve with the parsley or chilli flakes sprinkled over.

Time: 15 minutes | Amount: serves 2

Ingredients:

- ◆ 250ml gluten free oats
- ◆ 300g calamari, cleaned thinly sliced into rings
- ◆ 1 egg, beaten
- ◆ 1 lemon
- ◆ 15ml paprika
- ◆ 15ml parsley, chopped
- ◆ Salt and pepper for seasoning
- ◆ Preheat air fryer to 180ºC

Preparation:

1.	Place oats into a kitchen appliance like a food processor or blender and blitz up in pulses until the mixture resembles breadcrumbs.
2.	Place egg into a medium size bowl and oat crumbs into another. Season oats with sea salt and black pepper to taste, then add the paprika and the parsley.
3.	Place calamari rings onto a work surface and squeeze the fresh or bottled lemon juice over.
4.	Coat your hands with a bit of the crumbed oats to make them less tactile and then dip each calamari ring into the oat mix, then the egg mix, and finally the oat mix once more.
5.	Lightly shake off excess oats, place rings in one layer in the fryer basket, and cook for 8 or 10 minutes, giving them a toss halfway through.
6.	Serve the dish with lemon wedges and chips.
7.	Make sure the calamari are thinly sliced so that it cooks evenly and doesn't toughen.

Time: 30 minutes | Amount: serves 6

Ingredients:

- ♦ 300g mashed potatoes
- ♦ 300g fish of your choice
  – salmon, cod, haddock, hake
- ♦ 1 egg, beaten
- ♦ Seasoning
- ♦ 15ml Dijon mustard
- ♦ 15ml spring onion, sliced diagonally into pieces
- ♦ 125ml Panko breadcrumbs
- ♦ Cooking spray

Preparation:

1.	Combine fish, seasoning, and egg in a food processor by pulsing the mix 3 to 4 times until smooth.
2.	Place fish mix, mashed potatoes, and spring onion into a round bowl an combine together with a rubber spatula.
3.	Divide the mix into 6 evenly sized balls and press down until it forms a 2cm thick patty. Place breadcrumbs in a dish and dip the fish cakes in until coated on all sides.
4.	Cover and chill while you preheat the air fryer to 220°C. Remove fish cakes from fridge, and spray on both sides with cooking spray.
5.	Place cakes into the fryer basket in one layer and cook for 10 to 15 minutes, turning over halfway, until golden brown.
6.	Serve with a side salad or lightly boiled green beans.

Time: 30 minutes | Amount: serves 2

Ingredients:

- ♦ 8 large prawns, cleaned, shelled and deveined
- ♦ 250ml coconut milk
- ♦ 125g desiccated coconut
- ♦ 125ml Panko breadcrumbs
- ♦ 2ml cayenne pepper
- ♦ 1ml kosher salt
- ♦ 1ml black pepper
- ♦ 125ml marmalade
- ♦ 15ml honey
- ♦ 5ml mustard
- ♦ 2ml hot sauce
- ♦ Preheat air fryer to 180ºC

Preparation:

1.	Whisk the coconut milk and combine with the salt and the pepper. In another bowl, whisk the coconut, Panko, cayenne, and season the mix to taste.
2.	Dip the prawns into the coconut milk mix individually, and then place them in one layer into the air fryer basket.
3.	Cook for 22 minutes, turning halfway through. Check after 18 minutes to see how the cooking is progressing.
4.	While the prawns are in the air fryer, whisk together the honey, marmalade, mustard, and hot sauce.
5.	Serve the prawns with the sauce poured over immediately when they come out of the fryer.

Time: 20 minutes | Amount: serves 4

Ingredients:

- ♦ 4 cod, hake, or haddock fillets
- ♦ Seasoning
- ♦ 30ml flour
- ♦ 40g dried breadcrumbs
- ♦ Cooking spray
- ♦ 250g frozen peas
- ♦ 15ml Greek yogurt
- ♦ 12 capers
- ♦ Lemon juice
- ♦ 4 fresh, crispy bread rolls
- ♦ Preheat air fryer to 200ºC

Preparation:

1.	Season the fish fillets and lightly dust both sides with flour. Roll in breadcrumbs and shake off any excess crumbs.
2.	Lightly spray the base of fryer basket and place fillets in one layer to cook for 15 minutes.
3.	Cook peas in the microwave or stovetop for a few minutes while the fish is cooking. Drain the peas, add to a blender with the Greek yogurt, capers, and lemon juice. Blitz until creamy.
4.	Once the fish is cooked, layer the fillets onto the 4 buttered bread rolls individually and top with the pea sauce.
5.	Serve immediately.

Time: 15 minutes | Amount: serves 2

Ingredients:

♦ 2 fillets of fresh salmon

♦ Bottle of Cajun seasoning

♦ Lemon

♦ Heat up air fryer to 180ºC

Preparation:

1.	Pat salmon fillets dry and lightly dust with the Cajun seasoning (ensure all sides are coated). No other seasoning is required.
2.	For salmon fillets of about 2cm thick, airfry for 7 minutes, stopping halfway to turn them over.
3.	Serve salmon fillets when they are ready with a squeeze of fresh lemon juice.

Time: 15 minutes | Amount: serves 2

Ingredients:

- 4 fish fillets of your favourite white fish, deboned, and cut into 1cm thickness
- Lemon pepper
- Sea salt
- Freshly picked dill
- Lemon
- Preheat air fryer to 180°C

Preparation:

1.	Season fillets with lemon pepper, sea salt, and chopped dill sprinkled over both sides.
2.	Place the fish fillets into the air fryer basket on top of a parchment or baking sheet.
3.	Cut lemon into quarters and place around the fish.
4.	Cook for 7 to 8 minutes in the air fryer, checking after 5 or 6 minutes to see how well the fish is cooked.
5.	When the fish is soft and flaking easily with a knife, remove from the air fryer.
6.	Serve immediately with chips and more lemon.

Time: 40 minutes | Amount: serves 4

Ingredients:

- 500ml milk
- 2 bay leaves
- 1 onion, cut into quarters
- 4 whole cloves
- 3 potatoes
- Butter
- 25ml cornflour
- 80ml double cream
- 30ml chervil
- Seasoning
- Preheat air fryer to 200ºC

Preparation:

1.	Place haddock, milk, and bay leaves into a saucepan. Stud onion quarters with one clove each and place in saucepan with fish. Bring to boil while watching, and then simmer until the fish is cooked well and the flesh flakes easily with a fork. Remove fish with draining spoon and cool.
2.	Strain milk liquid and set aside.
3.	Peel the potatoes and slice them thinly. Bring a medium size saucepan of water to the boil on the stovetop and blanch potatoes for one to two minutes. Drain.
4.	Grease 4 small ramekins or one tin dish with butter. Layer the base with a third of the potato slices.
5.	Mix cornflour and a small amount of the milk mix it all to form a paste, then stir in the fresh cream and chervil. Next, gradually add the rest of the milk slowly and stir it until the sauce thickens. Add the flaked fish and coat well with sauce.
6.	Finish layering the dish with a fish layer, another layer of potato slices, a layer of fish, and then finish with a final layer of potatoes.
7.	Cook for 15 minutes, or until the potatoes are a golden brown, and the sauce is bubbling. Check dish at the 10 minute mark for doneness.

Ingredients:

- ◆ 1 x 500g bag fresh mussels direct from the seafood counter at your local fishmonger
- ◆ 50g butter
- ◆ 250ml water
- ◆ 2 – 3 crushed garlic cloves
- ◆ 5ml chives
- ◆ 5ml dried basil
- ◆ 5ml finely chopped parsley
- ◆ Preheat air fryer to 200ºC when mussels are prepped

Preparation:

1.	Put bag of mussels straight into the refrigerator until cooking time.
2.	Pick through the mussels and throw away any that are cracked. If you see any open mussels, give the shell a smart tap and throw it away if it doesn't close.
3.	Place mussels into a bowl of fresh water for about 30 minutes to rid them of grit.
4.	Scrub mussels with a brush before cooking to remove mussel "beards."
5.	Place mussels into an air fryer-safe pan with butter, water, garlic, and herbs.
6.	Set air fryer timer for 3 minutes to see if mussels have opened. The length of time the mussels cook for is according to the air fryer wattage, and how many mussels there are. Keep checking every 1 minute after the first 3 minutes of cooking.
7.	When they are all open, serve with a loaf of ciabatta or chips and mayonnaise.

Time: 40 minutes | Amount: serves 4

Ingredients:

- 15ml Panko breadcrumbs
- 30ml dried mixed herbs
- 5ml paprika
- 5ml salt
- 15ml olive oil
- 750g chicken breast, flattened to 1cm thickness
- 250ml drained corn kernels
- 250ml ripe strawberries
- 1 small round of fresh goat cheese, cubed
- 2 avocados, halved and cubed
- 2 lightly boiled hard boiled eggs
- 30ml canola or extra virgin olive oil
- 500g packet of baby kale greens, washed and ready to eat
- Preheat air fryer to 190ºC

Preparation:

1.	Combine Panko, herb, paprika, sea salt, and canola or olive oil in a small bowl. Apply mix to clean and dry chicken breasts on both sides.
2.	Cook chicken breasts in the air fryer for 20 minutes, turning over halfway through cooking. After the chicken breasts are perfectly cooked, set aside on a plate.
3.	Place the kale onto a rectangular plate, and lightly pour over some oil, and season the kale to taste. Put the corn kernels, strawberries, goat's cheese, avocados, and sliced chicken on top.
4.	Serve with extra olive oil and mayonnaise on the table.

Time: 50 minutes | Amount: Serves 2

Ingredients:

♦ 2 skinless chicken breasts, flattened out to 1cm thick

♦ 2 potatoes, washed and sliced lengthways

♦ 1 large packet rocket, washed and ready to eat

♦ Half a punnet of cherry tomatoes, sliced in half

♦ 1 chopped red onion

♦ Seasoning

♦ 3ml dried oregano, garlic powder, paprika, black pepper

♦ 15ml olive oil

♦ Preheat air fryer to 190ºC

Preparation:

1.	Coat air fryer basket and both sides of the cleaned and dried chicken breasts with cooking spray.
2.	Season the chicken to taste, place in the basket with a little space between the breasts, and cook for around15 to 20 minutes until cooked through. Keep warm.
3.	In the meantime, toss the potatoes in olive oil with the dried oregano, garlic powder, paprika, black pepper.
4.	When chicken has finished cooking, place the potatoes in one layer in the air fryer basket (cook in more batches if needed). Cooking time is 15 minutes a batch.
5.	When the potatoes are finished cooking, toss the tomatoes, the onion, and rocket together with a little bit of the olive oil, and put the hot potatoes on top to wilt the rocket. Slice the warm chicken into shreds, and scatter on top of the potatoes.
6.	Drizzle salad with more olive oil, season the dish to taste, and serve with ciabatta bread.

Time: 10 minutes | Amount: serves 4

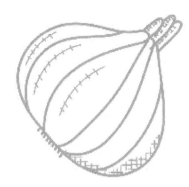

Ingredients:

♦ 3 slices whole grain bread

♦ 30ml extra virgin olive oil

♦ Garlic powder

♦ Salt to taste

♦ 1 packet mixed green salad leaves, washed and ready to use

♦ Half a punnet of cherry tomatoes, cut in half

♦ Half a cucumber, sliced

♦ 1 finely chopped onion

♦ Balsamic vinegar

♦ Extra virgin olive oil for dressing

♦ Preheat air fryer to 200ºC

Preparation:

1.	Cut bread into cubes and toss in the olive oil.
2.	Sprinkle cubes with garlic and salt.
3.	Place bread cubes into the fryer basket and then cook for 5 to 7minutes, depending how crispy you want your croutons.
4.	Combine the vegetable ingredients, mix balsamic vinegar and olive oil together for the dressing, and pour over when ready to serve.
5.	Add croutons to the salad at the table.

Time: 15 minutes | Amount: serves 2

Ingredients:

- ♦ 1 packet of washed and ready to eat salad greens
- ♦ Half a punnet of cherry tomatoes, cut in half
- ♦ 1 sachet of black Kalamata olives
- ♦ 1 green pepper, thinly sliced
- ♦ 30ml Olive oil
- ♦ 3ml dried mixed herbs
- ♦ 1 packet of halloumi cheese
- ♦ Cooking spray
- ♦ Preheat air fryer to 180°C

Preparation:

1.	Slice the halloumi cheese into medium widths, and spray on both sides with cooking spray.
2.	Spray the fryer basket and put the halloumi slices in the air fryer for 10 minutes, remembering to check on cooking after 5 minutes to see if golden.
3.	Meanwhile, mix together salad ingredients, mix olive oil and mixed herbs in a round bowl and then pour over salad.
4.	When halloumi slices are golden, remove from the air fryer and put the cheese on the salad.
5.	Serve immediately.

Time: 30 minutes | Amount: serves 2

Ingredients:

♦ 2 large packets of kale leaves

♦ 15ml olive oil

♦ 5ml soy sauce

♦ 5ml black or white sesame seeds, toasted

♦ 5ml dried, chopped garlic

♦ 2ml poppy seeds

♦ Preheat air fryer to 190ºC

Preparation:

1.	Wash kale and allow to dry. Tear leaves into medium size pieces. Toss olive oil, soy sauce, and kale together in a bowl. Make sure every leaf is covered in oil.
2.	Place one third of the leaves in a single layer into the air fryer basket. Cook for 6 minutes or until crisp, shaking the basket half way through. Take kale out and lay on a baking sheet. Sprinkle kale chips with sesame seeds, garlic, and poppy seeds.
3.	Repeat with the remaining kale.
4.	Serve kale chip salad with chops or grilled Portobello mushrooms.

Time: 40 minutes | Amount: serves 4

Ingredients:

- 4 flour tortillas
- 250ml grated cheese, divided into 4 portions
- 1 sliced bell pepper
- 4 sliced courgettes
- 1 tin black or other beans, drained, cleaned, and rinsed
- Cooking spray
- 1 tub Greek yogurt
- 5ml lime zest +juice from one or two limes
- 125ml chopped, fresh coriander leaves
- 1 jar of tomato salsa

Preparation:

1.	Preheat air fryer to 200°C
2.	Smooth out the tortillas onto a work surface. Sprinkle each with one-half of the cheese portion. Top each tortilla with one quarter of the bell pepper slices, courgette, and black beans. Sprinkle with again with remaining cheese.
3.	Fold tortillas to form the classic quesadilla shape. Next, lightly coat each quesadilla with non-stick spray, and secure each one with a toothpicks.
4.	Lightly spray fryer basket with non-stick spray. Carefully put quesadillas in the fryer basket (two at a time), and cook until the tortillas are golden, slightly crispy, and the cheese inside is melted. The vegetables must also be slightly softened (about 10 minutes). Remember to turn the quesadillas halfway through cooking time. Finish the batch of remaining quesadillas.
5.	While quesadillas are cooking, combine lime zest and juice, yogurt, and coriander leaves in a bowl.
6.	Serve quesadillas with yogurt dip and salsa.

Time: 1 hour 10 – 15 minutes approximately | Amount: serves 4

Ingredients:

- 2 packets firm tofu
- Cooking spray
- 1 orange, juiced
- 30ml soy sauce
- 30ml honey
- 3oml toasted sesame oil
- 5ml rice vinegar
- 3ml cornstarch
- 2 packets boil in the bag rice
- 3ml kosher salt
- 30ml chopped spring onions
- Toasted sesame seeds to serve

Preparation:

1.	Preheat air fryer to 180°C
2.	Place tofu on a plate with paper towels. Place more paper towels on top and allow to drain for 30 minutes. Coat with cooking spray.
3.	Place half tofu into fryer basket in one layer and then cook for around 15 minutes until lightly brown or golden, and crispy. Cook second batch and keep warm.
4.	Whisk together orange juice, soy sauce, honey, sesame oil, rice vinegar, cornstarch in a small pan over medium high heat. Whisking until brought to a brisk boil and thick. Set aside.
5.	Prepare rice. Toss tofu in sauce, and pour over rice.
6.	Season to taste, sprinkle with spring onions and serve.

Time: 45 minutes | Amount: serves 2 - 4

Ingredients:

- 2 packets baby spinach leaves
- Water
- 125ml cream cheese
- 125ml Feta cheese
- 30ml grated Parmesan cheese
- 1 egg white
- Lemon zest from one lemon
- 5ml dried oregano
- Seasoning
- 4 sheets Phyllo pastry, thawed out and kept under a damp cloth
- 15ml olive oil
- Cooking spray

Preparation:

1.	Wilt spinach in a wok with a bit of water. Drain and cool. Press with paper towels to remove excess water.
2.	Stir spinach, cheeses, egg white, zest, oregano, and sea salt and white pepper seasoning in a bowl until combined.
3.	Place one phyllo sheet on a work surface and brush lightly with olive oil. Top with second sheet and repeat until all 4 sheets are oiled and stacked.
4.	Cut sheets into 8 x 6cm strips and cut those strips in half. Spoon 15ml filling onto the narrow end of each strip and fold one corner down to envelope the filling and to form a triangle. Carry on folding in a triangle shape until the strip has turned into a triangle parcel. Continue this technique with remaining sheet strips and filling.
5.	Preheat air fryer to 190°C.
6.	Lightly coat air fryer basket with cooking spray. Place 8 spanakopita inside with the seam side down in the basket and cook until golden brown. Repeat until batches are finished.
7.	Serve warm with salad.

Time: 25 minutes | Amount: serves 2 - 4

Ingredients:

- ♦ 1 large cauliflower, rinsed, broken into bite-size florets
- ♦ 250ml flour
- ♦ 5ml vegan bouillon granules
- ♦ 2ml cayenne pepper
- ♦ 2ml chilli powder
- ♦ 2ml paprika
- ♦ 2ml dried chilli flakes
- ♦ 250ml almond, soy, or rice milk
- ♦ Canola oil spray
- ♦ 30ml margarine
- ♦ 125ml hot sauce
- ♦ 2 cloves garlic, crushed
- ♦ Preheat air fryer to 190°C

Preparation:

1.	Mix flour, granules, and spices together in a large bowl. Slowly whisk in milk until it forms a batter.
2.	Spray the fryer basket with non-stick spray.
3.	Toss the cauliflower florets in the batter mixture and transfer to the basket. Cook for 20 minutes, turning the florets after 10 minutes. Place the florets in a single layer, and you can cook in more than one batch if needed.
4.	Heat the margarine, hot sauce, and fresh garlic in a small saucepan on top of the stove. Bring the mix to boil and then simmer on lowest setting with the lid on.
5.	When florets are all cooked, transfer to a bowl, pour over the hot sauce, toss gently and serve immediately with a cool ranch dressing dip.

Time: 25 minutes | Amount: serves 2

Ingredients:

- ♦ 1 bag soy fingers
- ♦ 750ml boiling water
- ♦ 100ml finely ground cornmeal (or flour)
- ♦ 100ml Engevita nutritional yeast flakes
- ♦ 7.5ml chicken seasoning
- ♦ 5 – 10ml Cajun seasoning to taste
- ♦ Salt and pepper
- ♦ Preheat air fryer to 190ºC

Preparation:

1.	Place soy fingers in a pan and pour over boiling water. Allow to soak for around 10 minutes until softened.
2.	Drain soy fingers through a strainer and gently press out excess water with a wooden spoon.
3.	Mix flour, yeast flakes, and selected seasoning together in a small round bowl and then add the soy fingers. Coat each piece well and shake off any excess crumbs.
4.	Place fingers in fryer basket and fry for 5 minutes, shake the basket and immediately return to fryer for a further 5 minutes.
5.	Serve with mash potatoes and vegan gravy.

Time: 2 hours | Amount: 1 loaf serves 6

Ingredients:

- ◆ 450g all-purpose flour
- ◆ 75g butter
- ◆ 275ml full fat milk
- ◆ 30ml olive oil
- ◆ 30ml coconut oil
- ◆ ½ sachet instant yeast powder
- ◆ Salt

Preparation:

1.	Rub the room temperature butter into the all-purpose flour until it resembles fine crumbs.
2.	Warm the milk and oils up in a pan unitlike warm.
3.	Pour milk and oil mix into your bowl with the butter and flour, and combine together until it forms a dough.
4.	Knead for 5 minutes.
5.	Place a damp tea towel over the bread dough bowl, and rest in a warm place for one hour.
6.	Knock the dough back after one hour, and knead again. Leave the dough to prove in a warm spot for half an hour.
7.	Preheat air fryer to 185ºC.
8.	Shape the dough into round balls, and put, into a well-oiled air fryer pan. Make a ring of dough balls framing the edge of the pan, and then place in the middle. They must all be touching so the bread can be pulled apart after baking.
9.	Bake for 12 to 15 minutes.

Time: 30 minutes | Amount: serves 4

Ingredients:

- 8 slices of your favourite bread, multigrain is best
- 2 large boiled and mashed potatoes
- 5ml grated ginger
- 10ml coriander powder
- 5ml cumin powder
- 2.5ml chilli powder or flakes
- 2.5ml garam masala
- Salt to taste
- Bowl of water
- Cooking oil for brushing

Time: 10 minutes | Amount: 2 cocktails

Ingredients:

- 4 slices ciabatta bread
- 30ml to 60ml salted butter (depending on how buttery you like your garlic bread)
- 3 cloves crushed, fresh garlic
- Few pinches dried parsley
- 60ml grated parmesan cheese
- Preheat air fryer to 180ºC

Preparation:

1.	Place butter in small bowl and microwave for approximately 10 seconds until soft, not melted.
2.	Mix in the fresh garlic, chopped parsley, and cheese.
3.	Spread mix onto the ciabatta slices.
4.	Arrange the slices in the air fryer tray, and cook for around 5 minutes. Check after 3 minutes to see if it's ready.
5.	Serve while still hot with the hummus.

Time: 20 minutes | Amount: Serves 4

Ingredients:

- ◆ 4 bake-at-home bread rolls
- ◆ 100g room temperature butter
- ◆ 60ml freshly squeezed garlic cloves
- ◆ 75ml/30g each cheddar cheese, goat's cheese,
  mozzarella, Feta, and Edam
- ◆ 60ml chives
- ◆ Seasoning to taste

Preparation:

1.	Grate the hard cheeses, and finely dice the soft cheeses.
2.	Melt the butter medium heat setting, add the seasoning, chives, and garlic, simmer gently for 2 minutes, and take off the hob.
3.	Cut slits into the bake-at-home bread rolls, but don't slice through.
4.	Coat the slits on both sides with the garlic butter.
5.	Combine the cheeses together, and spoon the mixture into every alternate slit in the rolls.
6.	Place in the air fryer for 5 minutes, check half way through to see if the cheese is melting and the bread is crisping up.
7.	Serve with hot beef stock for dip

Time: 30 minutes | Amount: serves 4 as a side dish

Ingredients:

- ♦ 500g broccoli, rinsed and cut into bite size florets
- ♦ 7.5ml peanut oil
- ♦ 2 cloves crushed garlic
- ♦ Salt
- ♦ 30ml soy sauce
- ♦ 30ml honey or agave
- ♦ 15ml rice vinegar
- ♦ Asian chilli sauce (or Sriracha)
- ♦ 100ml salted peanuts
- ♦ Lime juice
- ♦ Preheat air fryer to 200°C

Preparation:

1.	Toss broccoli, oil, garlic and salt together. Make sure that every floret is coated with oil.
2.	Spread in one layer in the air fryer basket and cook in batches if needed.
3.	Cook for around 20 minutes, giving the basket a shake halfway through.
4.	Meanwhile, mix honey, soy sauce, chilli sauce (homemade if you have the time), and vinegar together in a round bowl and then microwave for10 to 15 seconds.
5.	Transfer cooked broccoli to a bowl and coat in sauce. Add a bit more salt if you prefer.
6.	Stir through peanuts and add a small squeeze of lime.
7.	Serve with a protein of your choice.

PALEO CHICKEN NUGGETS

Time: 25 minutes | Amount: serves 4

Ingredients:

- 500g boneless, skinless chicken breast
- 2ml salt
- 5ml sesame oil
- 100ml coconut flour
- 3ml ginger powder
- 4 egg whites
- 100ml toasted sesame seeds
- Cooking spray
- Preheat air fryer to 200ºC

Preparation:

1.	Cut dried and cleaned chicken breasts into bite size pieces, pat dry and put in a bowl. Toss with salt and sesame oil until coated on all sides.
2.	Place coconut flour and ginger into a Ziploc bag and shake to combine. Add chicken and coat on all sides.
3.	Put the egg whites in a large round bowl and add chicken. Toss chicken pieces in egg whites until well coated. Remove chicken from bowl, allow egg whites to drip off slightly, then sprinkle over the sesame seeds,
4.	Spray air fryer basket well with cooking spray and place chicken nuggets in a single layer in the basket. Make sure the pieces don't touch and cook in batches if needed.
5.	Cook for 6 minutes, remove nuggets from air fryer, turn nuggets over with a shake of the basket, and then return to the air fryer for another 6 minutes.
6.	Serve with dip.

Preparation:

1.	Place mash potato mix into a large round bowl and add spices.
2.	Combine ingredients until it is a smooth stuffing.
3.	Divide stuffing into 16 balls, and set aside.
4.	Place slice of bread onto chopping board and cut into rectangles. If preferred, you can remove the crusts.
5.	Put all the ingredients onto the work surface – water, stuffing, and bread.
6.	Pick up one bread slice rectangle and dip into the water very briefly.
7.	Place slice between palms of the hand, and gently squeeze out excess water.
8.	Place ball of stuffing in middle of slice, and roll the bread up around the stuffing like a carpet. Wrap very tightly so no stuffing is showing.
9.	Continue with rest of slices, placing on a plate when complete.
10.	Preheat sir fryer to 195ºC, and set the timer for 20 minutes which includes the preheating time.
11.	Meanwhile, brush a little oil onto stuffed bread rolls to prevent sticking to the air fryer basket.
12.	After 3 minutes of preheating, open the air fryer and place 6 to 8 rolls in the basket per batch.
13.	Air fry to 15 to 18 minutes until golden brown, checking half way.
14.	Serve with cheese sauce or tomato relish.

Time: 20 minutes | Amount: Makes 48

Ingredients:

- ♦ 4 egg whites at room temperature
- ♦ 125ml grated cheddar cheese
- ♦ 15ml water
- ♦ Seasoning to taste preference

Preparation:

1.	Spray two muffin pans with non-stick spray
2.	Heat up the air fryer to195ºC.
3.	Whisk egg whites, water, and seasoning until stiff peaks form.
4.	Spoon one tablespoon (about 30ml) into each individual muffin holder.
5.	Place one tray on the upper shelf and the other on the bottom shelf of the air fryer for 5 minutes. Then change them around by moving the top tray to the bottom, and vice versa. Bake for another 5 minutes, checking after 3 minutes. Make sure the bread chips do not over-brown.
6.	Remove from the muffin pan with a spatula, and then use the remainder of the mixture to repeat the process.
7.	Serve with hummus, relish, or dip.

Time: 15 minutes | Amount: serves 2 - 4

Ingredients:

♦ 10 fresh jalapeno peppers, deseeded and sliced in half vertically

♦ 175g low-fat cream cheese

♦ 125ml grated cheese of your choice

♦ 4 slices of bacon, grilled up until nicely crispy and crumbled

♦ Cooking spray

♦ Preheat air fryer to 180°C

Preparation:

1.	Place the cream cheese in a round bowl and microwave quickly for 10 to 15 seconds to soften.
2.	Combine cheeses together with the bacon bits and mix well.
3.	Stuff each jalapeno half with cream cheese mix.
4.	Load poppers into the air fryer basket and then spray well with cooking spray.
5.	Cook for around 5 minutes.
6.	Remove poppers from the basket and serve.

Time: 50 minutes | Amount: serves 4

Ingredients:

- ♦ 500g fresh salmon, skinned and cut finely
- ♦ 125ml mashed avocado
- ♦ 125ml coriander leaves, chopped
- ♦ 20ml curry powder
- ♦ 3ml sea salt
- ♦ 125ml tapioca starch + 20ml extra
- ♦ 125ml desiccated coconut
- ♦ Coconut oil for brushing

Preparation:

1.	Preheat air fryer to 200ºC
2.	Place salmon in large bowl and add the avocado, coriander leaves, salt, and curry powder and mix well. Add tapioca starch and mix.
3.	Place salmon cakes onto a medium size plate previously lined with baking parchment, and then freeze.
4.	While patties are in the freezer, rub the air fryer basket down with the coconut oil. Whisk up the eggs and pour them into a shallow plate. Place the 20ml extra tapioca starch and coconut flakes into a separate bowl.
5.	When patties have been in the freezer for 20 to 30 minutes, remove and dip each patty into the egg mix. Allow excess egg to drip off before dipping patty into the coconut mix. Coat on every side. Repeat the process with remaining patties.
6.	Brush the patties with a coconut oil, place in the basket, and cook for around 15 minutes.
7.	Serve with a fresh green garden salad.

Time: 25 minutes | Amount: serves 2 - 4

Ingredients:

- 1 large sweet potato
  (orange or white flesh),
  cut into small cubes
- 1fresh cauliflower,
  cut up into small bite-size florets
- 1 spring onion, diagonally chopped
- 2 cloves fresh garlic, crushed
- One small bunch of coriander leaves
- 60ml olive oil
- 2ml chilli powder
- 2ml cumin
- 60ml tapioca starch
- 60ml ground flaxseed
- 60ml each sunflower seeds + pumpkin
  seeds
- Seasoning
- Preheat air fryer to 180ºC

Preparation:

1.	Place sweet potato into food processor setup on a flat surface, and pulse until broken up.
2.	Add cauliflower, onion, and garlic and pulse again.
3.	Add seeds, starch, leaves from the coriander, and seasoning. Continue to pulse until a paste has formed.
4.	Scoop out small handfuls of the paste and form into patties one at a time. Put on a plate and chill for 10 minutes.
5.	Place in the basket (4 at a time) and cook for 18 to 20 minutes, flipping over halfway.
6.	Serve with green salad.

Time: 25 minutes | Amount: serves 2

Ingredients:

- ♦ 1 block extra firm tofu
- ♦ 60ml soy sauce
- ♦ 1 onion, chopped
- ♦ 4 carrots, diced
- ♦ 5ml turmeric
- ♦ 750ml riced cauliflower
- ♦ 60ml soy sauce
- ♦ 7,5ml sesame oil
- ♦ 30ml rice vinegar
- ♦ 15ml grated fresh ginger
- ♦ 1 finely grated broccoli floret
- ♦ 2 cloves crushed garlic
- ♦ 125ml frozen peas
- ♦ Preheat air fryer to 180ºC

Preparation:

1.	Place tofu in a large bowl and crumble into pieces, about the size of a £2 coin. Toss tofu pieces with soy sauce, onion, carrots, and turmeric.
2.	Put in basket and cook for around 10 minutes, shaking once halfway. Remove the tofu, and set aside.
3.	Mix cauliflower, the soy sauce, the sesame oil, and the rice vinegar, ginger, broccoli, garlic, and peas together in a large bowl. Place in air fryer basket and cook for 10 minutes, giving the basket a shake halfway through.
4.	Mix both bowls of ingredients together and serve with a fresh green salad.

Time: 15 minutes | Amount: serves 2 - 4

Ingredients:

- 1kg large prawns, cooked, peeled, and deveined
- 4 cloves rushed garlic
- 200ml grated Parmesan
- 5ml black pepper
- 3ml oregano
- 5ml dried basil
- 5ml onion powder
- 60ml olive oil
- 1 lemon

Preparation:

1.	Preheat air fryer to 180°C
2.	Place garlic, parmesan, pepper, oregano, basil, the onion powder, and the oil in a bowl, and then mix well.
3.	Gently toss prawns in the mix until well coated.
4.	Spray air fryer basket with cooking spray and place prawns in one layer.
5.	Cook for around 8 to 10 minutes until crispy and golden. Cook up in batches if needed.
6.	Serve with lemon wedges.

Time: 50 minutes | Amount: serves 2 - 4

Ingredients:

- ◆ 500g cubed venison, ostrich, or beef steak
- ◆ 1 egg, beaten
- ◆ 125ml grated parmesan
- ◆ 125ml pork scratchings, crumbed
- ◆ Cooking spray

Preparation:

1.	Combine pork scratchings and parmesan together and set aside.
2.	Place egg in a bowl. Dip meat cubes individually into the egg mix first, and then place into the crumb mix. Put onto a plate and freeze all the cubes for 30 minutes.
3.	Preheat air fryer to 175ºC. Take nuggets out of the freezer and spray all over with cooking spray.
4.	Spray air fryer basket with cooking spray, place in nuggets, and cook until brown for around 10 – 22 minutes, depending on whether you prefer your meat well-cooked or medium rare.
5.	Serve with a fresh green garden salad and low carb dip.
6.	Turn frittata onto a serving dish and decorate with rocket and tomato relish.

Time: 25 minutes | Amount: serves 2 - 4

Ingredients:

♦ 500g mince beef

♦ 2 eggs, beaten

♦ One onion, finely chopped

♦ One clove garlic, crushed

♦ 125ml almond flour

♦ 80ml coconut flour

♦ 125ml tomato sauce like Heinz

♦ Seasoning to taste

♦ 30ml Worcestershire sauce

♦ 5ml dried mixed herbs

♦ Preheat air fryer to 180°C

Preparation:

1.	Put all the ingredients into a round bowl and mix up well.
2.	Make patties about 6cm in diameter and 2cm thick, refrigerate for 10 minutes.
3.	Place the chilled patties in a single layer into the air fryer basket that has been sprayed well with cooking spray. Cook two batches if necessary.
4.	Cook for around 10 minutes, checking the patties halfway through the cooking time.
5.	Serve sliders, with mayonnaise and lettuce on your favourite low carb bread or rolls.

Time: 50 minutes | Amount: serves 4

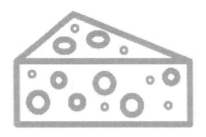

Ingredients:

- 125g cream cheese
- 250ml grated cheddar cheese
- 125ml grated parmesan cheese
- 125ml crushed pork scratchings

Preparation:

1.	Mix cream cheese in a large round bowl until it is smooth and creamy.
2.	Add grated cheddar cheese and combine.
3.	Form into evenly-sized balls, approximately the size of a £2 coin.
4.	Mix parmesan and pork scratchings together in a bowl and dip in cheese balls until evenly coated.
5.	Freeze balls for 30 mins until firm.
6.	Heat air fryer to 150ºC.
7.	Place balls into air fryer basket that has been sprayed with cooking spray. Cook balls for 2 to 3 minutes before checking for doneness. Remove from air fryer when balls are just melted inside.
8.	Serve with dip and green salad.

The opinions and ideas of the author contained in this publication are designed to educate the reader in an informative and helpful manner. While we accept that the instructions will not suit every reader, it is only to be expected that the recipes might not gel with everyone. Use the book responsibly and at your own risk. This work with all its contents, does not guarantee correctness, completion, quality or correctness of the provided information. Always check with your medical practitioner should you be unsure whether to follow a low carb eating plan. Misinformation or misprints cannot be completely eliminated. Human error is real!

Picture:Tatiana Bralnina // www.shutterstock.com

Design: Natalia Design

Printed in Great Britain
by Amazon